Contents

Any words appearing in bold, **like this**, are explained in the Glossary.

Ireland

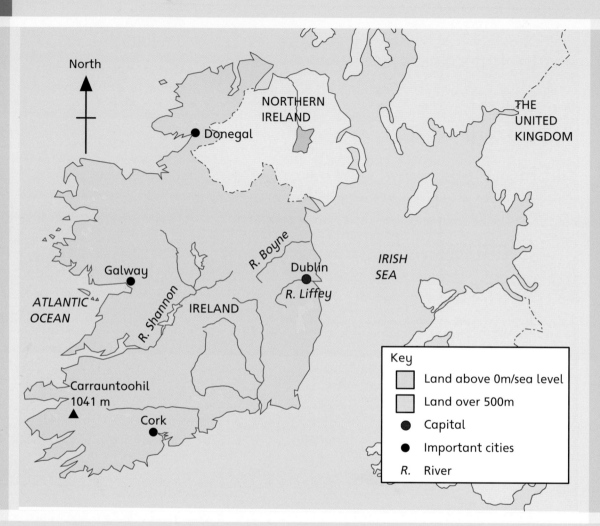

North

NORTHERN
IRELAND

THE
UNITED
KINGDOM

● Donegal

R. Boyne

Galway

Dublin

IRISH
SEA

R. Liffey

ATLANTIC
OCEAN

R. Shannon

IRELAND

Carrauntoohil
1041 m
▲

Cork

Key

Land above 0m/sea level

Land over 500m

● Capital

● Important cities

R. River

Ireland is in northern **Europe**. The north-east corner of the island is called Northern Ireland. Northern Ireland is part of the United Kingdom. The rest of the island is called the Republic of Ireland.

In the Republic of Ireland, most people live spread out around the country. About one and a half million people live in or around Dublin, the **capital**.

The city of Dublin is on the River Liffey.

Land

The centre of the Repubic of Ireland is low, flat farmland and **bog**. There are mountains around the coast. These beautiful, rounded mountains are not very high.

The land looks green all year round because it has so much rain. Winds bring clouds from the Atlantic Ocean. These drop rain as soon as they reach the Republic of Ireland.

Ireland is often called 'The Emerald Isle'. Emeralds are beautiful, green stones.

Landmarks

There are many **ancient** graves around the Republic of Ireland. The most famous one is at Newgrange. It is over 5,000 years old.

The name Burren is from an Irish word meaning a stony place.

The Burren is in the west of the Republic of Ireland. It is a huge, windswept area of rock with underground caves. There is nowhere else like it in all of **Europe**.

Homes

There are still a few **traditional** cottages. These are built from stone and have just one room. They have **thatched** roofs and a plot of land for growing food.

About 150 years ago, cruel landowners forced most people to move off their land to towns or overseas. Today many people live in modern houses in towns.

Food

Irish people usually eat their main meal in the evening. It might be Dublin coddle, a stew of sausages, bacon, onions and potatoes.

These fishing boats are in Killybegs, one of Ireland's most famous fishing towns.

Traditionally, the Republic of Ireland makes a lot of different breads and potato dishes. The **dairies** make very good cheeses. There is also lots of fresh seafood.

13

Clothes

The Republic of Ireland is famous for its **textiles**. Wool is woven into beautiful clothes. You can still buy handmade Aran jumpers from Galway, or beautiful **tweed** from Donegal.

Top designers display their clothes on catwalks, like this one.

In the last few years, some top **fashion designers** have moved to Dublin. Business is good for new designers and shops.

15

Work

Many farms are still small and people grow just enough food for themselves. In the west, there are beef and **dairy** farms. **Crops** grow better in the east, where it is not so wet.

Many people work in **factories**, making food or drink, like Guinness, the famous Irish beer. Glass, computers, metals, chemicals and **textiles** are also made.

Transport

It is easy to travel to and from other countries by sea or air. The Republic of Ireland has three **international** airports, and its own airline, Aer Lingus.

The Dart train route travels along part of the east coast of Ireland.

Most people in the Republic of Ireland travel by car. There are also trains, buses and trams.

Languages

English and Irish are the two **official** languages of the Republic of Ireland. The Irish language was brought to Ireland over 1,000 years ago by people from Eastern **Europe**.

INIS CIONAITH
WATERFALL

km *Cill Mocheanóg*
3 KILMACANOGE

Gleann Crí km
GLENCREE 13

Road signs are witten in English and Irish.

Everyone learns Irish at school. Some people in the west of Ireland still speak Irish as their main language.

School

Children go to primary school between the ages of 6 and 12. The day starts at nine in the morning and finishes at about three in the afternoon.

Most Irish students learn English, Irish and Maths, as well as other subjects.

Students have to go to secondary school from the age of 12 to 15. Their days are longer and they have more homework.

Free time

Many Irish people enjoy watching or playing sport. Race meetings attract huge crowds. Many young people keep their own ponies, even in the cities!

On Sunday, some families watch their local teams play **traditional** games. In **Gaelic** football, the players are allowed to hold the ball.

Hurling is a fast game played with a stick and ball.

Celebrations

The Irish Derby at Kildare is usually held in June. It is an important day for many Irish people. Horses from all around the world take part in the race.

Girls often wear beautiful, white dresses for their first communion.

A special day for every **Catholic** child is their First **Communion**. Everyone goes to church in their best clothes. Each child chooses a saint's name to add to their own.

The Arts

Long ago, each Irish village had its own storyteller. Some of their stories were written down in beautiful books. The Republic of Ireland has produced many famous writers.

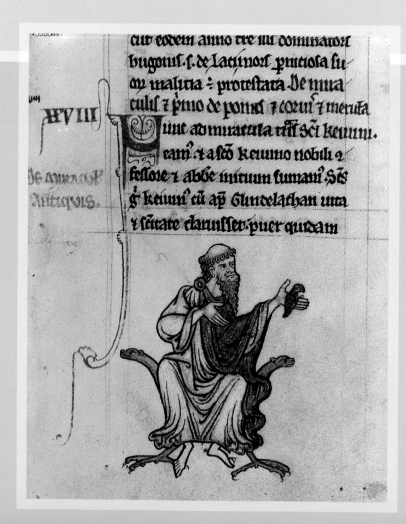

Musicans often play dance tunes and old **Gaelic** songs.

Almost every village has a **traditional** music group. People play the fiddle, the tin whistle, the uilleann pipes and the bodhrán (a small goatskin drum).

Factfile

Name	The full name of Ireland is the Republic of Ireland.
Capital	The **capital** city is Dublin.
Language	**Gaelic** Irish and English are the two **official** languages of the Republic of Ireland.
Population	There are about four million people living in the Republic of Ireland.
Money	Irish money is called the euro.
Religions	Almost all Irish people are **Catholics**. About 3 out of every 100 people are **Protestant**.
Products	The Republic of Ireland produces wheat, barley, potatoes, milk, **livestock**, beer, machinery and transport equipment.

Words you can learn

aon (ayn)	one
dó (doe)	two
trí (three)	three
tá (thaw)	yes
níl (knee)	no
dia dhuit (dee-a-gwit)	hello
slán agat (slawn-aguth)	goodbye
le do thoil (le-do-hull)	please

Glossary

ancient from a long time ago

bog land that is always wet and spongy

capital the city where the government is based

Catholic Christians who have the Pope in Rome as the head of their Church

Communion the Christian ceremony of eating bread and wine

crops the plants that farmers grow and harvest (gather)

dairies/dairy the type of farm that produces milk, cheese and yoghurt

Europe the collection of countries north of the Mediterranean Sea

factories buildings where something is made in large amounts.

fashion designers people who draw ideas for, and make, clothes

Gaelic the **ancient** language of the people who first lived in Ireland, Scotland, Wales and Breton, or describing anything that belonged to them

international to do with countries all around the World, not just Ireland

livestock animals kept on a farm for their meat or milk

official decided by the government

Protestant Christians who do not have the Pope as the head of their Church

textiles cloths or fabrics

thatched roofs made from thick layers of straw or reeds

traditional the way things have been done or made for a long time

tweed a thick, woven, wool fabric

Index